SHOW ME JESUS CHRIST

BOYS' DEVOTIONAL
FOR AGES 08 TO 12

BY

ANDERS BENNETT

Table of Contents

The Bible is one big book that is telling one main story. The whole thing is about how God loves us so much that He sent His Son, Jesus, to save us. What we're going to do together in this book is look for Jesus in every story. Jesus may be the main character in the story, or He may be hidden in the details. Wherever He is, we will ask God to "Show Me Jesus" while we study the Bible together. Before you begin reading each day, say this prayer.

I want to see Jesus on every page of
the Bible. I know the whole book is about Him.
Help me to understand who He is and what He
has done for me. Show me Jesus. Amen.

1. Creation

"And God saw everything that he had made, and behold, it was very good. And there was evening and there was morning, the sixth day." - Genesis 1:31

In the beginning, there was nothing and no one except for God. Can you imagine that? No earth to live on. No air to breathe. Nothing. Then one day, God decided to create absolutely everything. By simply speaking, God made everything. When He said, "Let there be light," there was light. When He said, "Let there be birds and fish," there they were.

But the most wonderful thing about God creating the world is how He saw it. He looked at everything that He had made and said that it was good. When God looks at you, He is proud and says that you are good, too. You're special because God made you and has called you good. God does not make mistakes. If you're ever unhappy with something about you, remember that God made you exactly how He wanted you.

Dear God, thank you for making me and calling me good. Help me to remember that you made me exactly how you want me to be. Amen.

2. Adam and Eve

"Then the Lord God formed the man of dust from the ground and breathed into his nostrils the breath of life, and the man became a living creature." - Genesis 2:7

Out of everything that God made, He made man a little differently. When God wanted to make the earth, He just said it. But when He made people, he took some of the dirt of the earth and breathed life into it. Imagine taking a handful of dust and blowing into it. When we do that, the dust scatters all around. But when God did it, it fell into place and made one of us.

God is a master creator. Our creativity comes from Him. The Bible says that it is a reflection of who He is. So when we're being creative, we're being like God. I want to encourage you to be creative today. Draw something new or make a new kind of snack. Enjoy all of the different things God has made and put them together in a new way.

Dear God, I am amazed at your creativity and power. I want to reflect on your glory this week while I make something new and creative. Amen.

3. The Sneaky Snake

"Now the serpent was more crafty than any other beast of the field that the Lord God had made. He said to the woman, "Did God actually say, 'You shall not eat of any tree in the garden'?" - Genesis 3:1

Adam and Eve had one rule to follow when living in God's perfect garden. This garden was full and beautiful. It was filled with all kinds of trees, bushes, and plants that had terrific fruit to choose from. But they were not allowed to eat the fruit from one tree in the garden.

The devil came to earth disguised as a snake and slithered his way up to Adam and Eve. He wanted them to question what God had said. And so, he asked a few questions that put doubt in their minds. Then Adam and Eve broke God's rule. Because God is perfect and holy, He couldn't let Adam and Eve stay in His perfect garden anymore. So He kicked them out. But what we will see is that He already had a plan to bring them back in.

Dear God, I have broken Your rules like Adam and Eve. Please forgive me for my sins. Amen.

4. Cain and Abel

"Cain spoke to Abel, his brother. And when they were in the field, Cain rose up against his brother Abel and killed him."
- Genesis 4:8

After Adam and Eve were kicked out of the garden, they started a family. They had two sons named Cain and Abel. Unfortunately, those sons were infected with the curse of sin that Adam and Eve had, too. Cain got so angry at Abel one day that he killed his own brother. The problem of sin had not stopped with Adam and Eve. It had grown and become worse.

Just like in the garden, God did not let the sin go unpunished. He sent Cain away from his family to start his own family somewhere else. God was protecting His people from sinful people that did not want to follow Him. Already, God is working to save His people from their sin and the sinful acts of other people.

Dear God, thank You for loving me and working to save me from my sin. Amen.

5. Noah's Ark

"Noah was a righteous man, blameless in his generation. Noah walked with God." - Genesis 6:9

Sin had infected everything and everyone in the world that God had created. He was so upset by this that He wanted to start over. He looked over all the people and only saw wicked and hateful people. But then He saw Noah. He saw that Noah and his family were trying their best to love and follow God. Although their actions were imperfect, their hearts were full of faith.

God told Noah to build a really big boat called an ark. He told Noah to take his family and some of all of the different kinds of animals and pile them on the boat. He was going to send a flood that would cover the whole earth. If they were on the ark, they would be saved. This story shows us God's desire to save those who have faith in Him. Jesus is like our ark. He has saved us from the punishment from God.

Dear God, I want to have faith like Noah. Make it clear to me what You want me to do for You. Amen.

6. Tower of Babel

"Then they said, "Come, let us build ourselves a city and a tower with its top in the heavens, and let us make a name for ourselves, lest we be dispersed over the face of the whole earth." - Genesis 11:4

Noah and his family lived under the promised blessing of God as they loved Him and He protected them. After many years that family passed away, and a new generation of people was born. These people turned away from God. They relied only on themselves for what they needed. They thought they were so smart and strong that they wanted everyone to know it. So they decided to build the world's tallest tower and biggest city.

God saw what they were doing and was saddened. They were trying to live life without Him, and He knew that they couldn't do that. He came down to see their tower. When He saw it, He decided to confuse their languages so they couldn't work together easily anymore. So they scattered and had to choose to rely on God or try to figure things out by themselves again.

Dear God, You know how life works best. Teach me to trust that I need You, and I can't do it all on my own. Amen.

7. The Promise

"I will bless those who bless you, and him who dishonors you I will curse, and in you all the families of the earth shall be blessed." - Genesis 12:3

After the tower of Babel, people spread over the world and started tribes, which grew to cities, which grew to countries. The world was full of all types of people. One of those people was named Abram. God chose Abram to be the start of His new people. He made a promise to Abram. He said the He would turn Abram into a great nation, give him a big piece of land to live on, and that all the people of the world would be blessed through Abram's family.

We don't know why God chose Abram. There was nothing special about him. He wasn't a king. He didn't have a lot of money. He was just a guy that God decided to set a special kind of love on. Because God did that, all people would be able to know Him. The promised blessing that was to come from Abram was Jesus, many years later.

Dear God, I am glad that I don't have to be rich or famous in order for You to love me. Thank You for choosing to love me. Amen.

8. The Promised Child

"The Lord visited Sarah as he had said, and the Lord did to Sarah as he had promised. And Sarah conceived and bore Abraham a son in his old age at the time of which God had spoken to him." - Genesis 21:1-2

Part of God's promise to Abram was that He was going to make Abram into a great nation. There was a problem, though. Abram didn't have any kids. And there was another problem. Abram and Sarah were really old, way too old to have kids. When God told Abram about this promise, Sarah overheard and laughed. She knew there was no way that she could have a baby.

But God is more powerful than we can even think, and He made a miracle happen. A year later, Sarah and Abram (whose name was changed to Abraham) had a baby boy named Isaac. God was beginning to keep these great big promises He had made to them. He began His new nation with this miraculous birth. Years later, with the miraculous birth of Jesus, He would start His church.

Dear God, You can do anything You want. Forgive me when I forget just how strong and powerful You are. Amen.

9. The Scariest Command

"He said, "Do not lay your hand on the boy or do anything to him, for now I know that you fear God, seeing you have not withheld your son, your only son, from me." - Genesis 22:12

Isaac was growing, and Abraham was learning what it meant to follow God. One day God gave Abraham the scariest command. He told Abraham to take his son, some wood, a torch, and a knife and go to the top of a mount. He told Abraham to sacrifice his son there. This was horrible. God had given Abraham this miraculous child, and now He wanted Abraham to kill him? This didn't make any sense.

But God never wanted Abraham to kill his son. You see, God had a ram on top of the hill ready to be sacrificed in his place. He just wanted to test Abraham's faith. And Abraham believed that God would raise Isaac from the dead. So, he went to offer him as a sacrifice. But right before he brought the knife down, God stopped him and showed him the ram. Isaac is a picture of Jesus for us. God didn't need Abraham to sacrifice Isaac because He was going to send His own Son, Jesus, as a sacrifice for all people.

Dear God, thank You for sacrificing Your Son for me. Your love for me is amazing. Amen.

10. Isaac Gets Married

"Then Isaac brought her into the tent of Sarah, his mother and took Rebekah, and she became his wife, and he loved her." - Genesis 24:67

Isaac's childhood was different from most children's when he grew up. He grew up moving around. Remember the promise that God made Abraham? God told Abraham that He would give him a land to live on. So, Abraham and his family moved closer and closer to that land. This move made it hard for Isaac to find a wife when he got older, but God had a plan.

God told him to send a servant to the nearest well. There he would meet a woman who would offer to get water out of the well for him and his camels. And so the servant went and prayed by the well. He asked God to send that woman. And before he could finish praying, there she was. Her name was Rebekah. God has sent her to the well at the exact right time. She came back to Abraham's house later and married Isaac.

Dear God, You have a wonderful plan for my life. Help me to trust that You know what's best. Amen.

"And the Lord said to her, "Two nations are in your womb, and two peoples from within you shall be divided; the one shall be stronger than the other, the older shall serve the younger." - Genesis 25:23

Isaac and Rebekah prayed that God would give them children, and God answered their prayer. While Rebekah was pregnant, she could feel a struggle within her. This struggle was the twin boys that she was going to have. God had something important to say about these two boys. Remember the nation that God promised Abraham, Isaac's dad? God promised that two nations were going to come out of those two boys.

They were going to be divided. They would end up enemies. One of the boys would be a part of the nation of God's people, and the other would be a part of that nation of God's enemies. Sometimes God does things that we don't understand. Sometimes He allows things that we don't agree with. What do we do then? We have to trust that God has a bigger plan.

Dear God, I do not understand everything You did in the Bible and why You do what You do now. I do know that You are trustworthy. Help me to trust You. Amen.

12. Jacob Tricks Isaac

"Jacob said to his father, "I am Esau, your firstborn. I have done as you told me; now sit up and eat of my game, that your soul may bless me." - Genesis 27:19

The twin boys that Isaac and Rebekah had were named Jacob and Esau. And from the very beginning, they were fighting one another. Jacob came out of the womb holding onto Esau's foot. After they grew up, Jacob tricked Esau into giving him his birthright over a bowl of soup. What's worse is that Jacob even tricked Isaac with his mom's help.

Isaac was getting really old and was about to die. So Jacob and Esau were going to go see him. Esau was supposed to get a blessing from Isaac. However, before he could, Rebekah told Jacob to dress up like Isaac and trick his dad into giving him the blessing. Because Isaac couldn't see very well, Jacob was able to trick him. A lifetime of tricks and fighting lead to a split in their family between Jacob and Esau, just as God had said.

Dear God, help me to live at peace with all of the people in my family. Amen.

13. Jacob's Ladder

"And he dreamed, and behold, there was a ladder set up on the earth, and the top of it reached to heaven. And behold, the angels of God were ascending and descending on it!"
- Genesis 28:12

Two incredible things happen on the night that Jacob had this dream. The first is the dream itself. Jacob dreamed that he saw a ladder that reached all the way to Heaven. Can you imagine what that would have looked like? Or how hard would that have been to climb? Jacob saw the angels going up and down that ladder and God standing at the top, speaking. This is the second amazing thing.

God made the same promise to Jacob that He had made to Abraham. He promised to make him into a great nation, gave a great land, and be a great blessing to all of the families on the earth. God was still going to use Jacob even after he was fighting with his brother and tricked his father. God uses imperfect people in His perfect plan.

Dear God, I am thankful that You use imperfect people like me. Thank You for letting me be a part of Your big story. Amen.

"And the messengers returned to Jacob, saying, "We came to your brother Esau, and he is coming to meet you, and there are four hundred men with him." - Genesis 32:6

Jacob and his brother, Esau, grew up and grew apart. They both started their own families and began growing those nations that God had promised them. One day when Jacob was traveling, he heard that Esau was coming his way with 400 people. Jacob that he was surly in for a fight. It was a fight that he could not win. So he decided to try to be so kind that Esau may forgive him for all the tricks he played on him.

Ahead of him, Jacob sent many gifts and half of the people he was traveling with. Eventually, Jacob had to face Esau. Instead of a fight, he was warmly embraced and forgiven. It wasn't the gifts that made Esau forgive Jacob. It was his love for his brother. God used that love to bring about forgiveness and keep Jacob safe.

Dear God, I need to forgive someone in my family for how they have treated me. Help me to do that. Amen.

15. Robe of Many Colors

"Now Israel loved Joseph more than any other of his sons, because he was the son of his old age. And he made him a robe of many colors". - Genesis 37:3

Jacob's family began to grow. In fact, he had 12 sons. If you've got brothers and sisters, then you know that there are good days and bad days in your family. Hopefully, though, you don't have a dad who has declared only one of the children his favorite child. This is what Jacob (now called Israel) did for his son, Joseph.

Not only was it known to the whole family that Joseph was the favorite, but he made him a colorful robe so that everyone would know. This obviously made all of his brothers furious, and rightly so. In God's family, we are all brothers and sisters, but He has not chosen a favorite son. In fact, He sent His own Son to die for all of us. We have a good Heavenly Father.

Dear God, I am so glad that you are a good Father to me. Show me how to forgive my father when he makes mistakes. Amen.

16. Betrayed By Brothers

"Come now, let us kill him and throw him into one of the pits. Then we will say that a fierce animal has devoured him, and we will see what will become of his dreams." - Genesis 37:20

Already disliked by his brothers, Joseph made matters worse when he told them about a dream he had. He dreamed that his whole family, including his mom and dad, would bow to him one day. When he told his brothers about this, they were furious. Not long after that, they were working in the field when Joseph came up. As he approached them, the brother decided to capture him and throw him into a pit. They were going to leave him for dead.

Right after throwing him in the pit, a group of people came by looking to buy a servant. So his brothers sold him to be a slave in a distant country. Joseph was beaten and betrayed by his own brothers. This gives us a glimpse of what Jesus would one day endure. He, too, would be beaten and betrayed by those who should have loved Him.

Dear God, when I am treated poorly, help me to remember Jesus. If He endured it, He can strengthen me too. Amen.

17. Potiphar's Palace

"And as soon as she saw that he had left his garment in her hand and had fled out of the house. "- Genesis 39:13

Joseph was sold to be a servant at Potiphar's palace. Potiphar had plenty of servants and a lot of jobs that had to be taken care of. Joseph did such a good job at the smaller tasks that he eventually became deeply trusted by Potiphar. He was given the most important jobs to take care of. Potiphar loved having Joseph around.
But Potiphar's wife wanted to take advantage of Joseph. She tempted him to sin with her. But Joseph said that he would not betray Potiphar or God for her. So he ran away so fast that he left his coat in her hands. Joseph may have made mistakes with his family, but he wasn't going to mess things up in this new position. We should be like Joseph and run away when we are tempted to do something that will displease God.

Dear God, give me the strength to run away from sin when I am tempted towards it. Amen.

18. Jail Cell Dreams

Potiphar had Joseph thrown in prison after the false accusations that his wife made about Joseph. There Joseph sat alone and betrayed once again. Sometime after that, the Pharaoh of Egypt tossed his cupbearer and baker into prison too. There they had dreams that they couldn't understand. When they told Joseph about those dreams, he said that God could help them understand.

God told Joseph that those dreams were about their future, that they would be let out of prison to stand before Pharoah again. The cupbearer would be restored, and the baker would be executed. In three days, these things happened just like Joseph said. He asked them to tell the Pharaoh about him, but they forgot about him. The beautiful thing this reminds us of is that God will never forget or abandon us.

Dear God, I am amazed that you will never leave me or forget me, even when I make mistakes. Amen.

19. Pharaoh's Dream

"Then Joseph said to Pharaoh, "The dreams of Pharaoh are one; God has revealed to Pharaoh what he is about to do." - Genesis 41:25

The cupbearer forgot about Joseph for two whole years. One day the Pharaoh had two crazy dreams that he couldn't understand. While he was talking about it, he remembered that Joseph had helped him understand his dream while he was in prison. So, Pharaoh called Joseph in and told him his dreams.

He dreamed that there was a herd of cattle and fields of grain that were strong and healthy-looking. Then came up a herd of ugly, skinny cattle and a withered field of grain that ate the healthy ones. By God's help, Joseph explained that God was saying there would be seven healthy years and seven withered years in Egypt. Pharaoh was so thankful and impressed by Joseph that he took him as his own servant.

Dear God, You can help me to understand difficult things, too. Help me to look to You for help. Amen.

20. Joseph's Family Reunion

"And now do not be distressed or angry with yourselves because you sold me here, for God sent me before you to preserve life." - Genesis 45:5

The seven healthy years were gone, and the seven withered years had begun. This made people from all over go to Egypt in order to get food that Joseph had helped Pharaoh store. One of the families that needed food was Isaac, Rebekah, and their 11 sons. Isaac told his sons to go and get some food from Egypt. When they arrived, Joseph recognized them immediately, but they did not recognize him. They probably thought he was still a servant in the middle of nowhere.

When Joseph told them who he was, they were terrified. They thought he would punish them or put them in jail. But Joseph showed them mercy. He said that God had a bigger plan for his life and used their meanness for everyone's good. Jesus does the same for us. He shows us mercy, and God used His death for our good.

Dear God, I will never deserve your mercy. Thank You for giving it to me freely. Amen.

21. Moses' Birth

"When the child grew older, she brought him to Pharaoh's daughter, and he became her son. She named him Moses, "Because," she said, "I drew him out of the water."
- Exodus 2:10

God's people lived in Egypt for a really long time. So long that people forgot all about Joseph and his family. There was a new Pharaoh in charge who did not like God's people. He was scared that they might want to be in charge one day. So he came up with a plan. He made a rule that any baby boy who was born in God's people was supposed to be thrown into the Nile River. How cruel is that!

God protected His people through this command. And one of the little boys that God saved was named Moses. God worked everything out that Moses was found in the Nile River. He wasn't dead but floating in a basket. He was found by none other than Pharaoh's daughter. She loved him and took him as his own. Moses would grow up to lead God's people out of Egypt. We will learn about that soon.

Dear God, You are in control of all things, and You alone can keep me truly safe. Amen.

22. Moses Runs Away

"When Pharaoh heard of it, he sought to kill Moses. But Moses fled from Pharaoh and stayed in the land of Midian. And he sat down by a well." - Exodus 2:15

When Moses grew older, he went outside one day and saw a fight. It was a small fight between an Egyptian and one of God's people. Moses got so mad that he went over and killed the Egyptian and hid him in the sand. Sounds like Moses was acting more like Pharaoh than God. One of God's people saw Moses do this and called him out for it.

Moses got scared and ran far away to a town called Midian. He sat down by a well and waited. He sat and thought about what he was going to do next. What could he do? He left God's people, and he left his family. It felt like he had to start over. But Moses wasn't alone in Midian. He could not run away from God. God found him and helped him to start over.

Dear God, I am so glad that I cannot run away from You forever. You will always find me. Amen.

23. Moses and the Burning Bush

"When Pharaoh heard of it, he sought to kill Moses. But Moses fled from Pharaoh and stayed in the land of Midian. And he sat down by a well. "- Exodus 3:4

One day, when Moses was out being a shepherd in Midian, he saw something very strange. He saw a bush that had caught on fire. And if that wasn't strange enough, the bush wasn't burning up. It was one fire, but not a single leaf was singed. How could this happen? God had made this happen to get Moses' attention, and it worked.

God called to Moses from the burning bush because He wanted to talk to him. God told Moses that He wanted him to be the leader of His people. He was going to use Moses to free His people from the Egyptians. Moses was so scared and tried to make excuses why he was not a good enough leader. And God agreed. Moses was not a good enough leader, but God was a good enough God. And that's all that mattered.

Dear God, sometimes You will ask me to do hard and scary things. I will trust You when You do. Amen.

24. Moses and the 10 Plagues

"The Egyptians shall know that I am the Lord, when I stretch out my hand against Egypt and bring out the people of Israel from among them." - Exodus 7:5

God gave Moses a friend named Aaron who would help him lead God's people. This was the plan. They were supposed to march up to Pharaoh and tell him to let God's people go. If he didn't, then there would be consequences. The consequences were that God would send ten different plagues on the Egyptian people. When Moses and Aaron told Pharaoh about this, he didn't listen. He didn't believe that God could do that.

But that is exactly what God did. He sent plagues like frogs, boils, gnats, rivers of blood, and even darkness to show His power over the Egyptians. Each time, God gave Pharaoh another chance to let His people go. And every time, Pharaoh did not listen to God. Finally, God sent the last, most terrible plague. God said that if they would sacrifice a lamb and paint their doors with its blood, then their sons would be kept safe from death. But Pharaoh and the Egyptians did not believe in God. That night, after everyone went to bed, all the firstborn sons in Egypt died because they did not believe in God.

> **Dear God, thank You for giving me so many chances to believe in You. You are so patient with me. Amen.**

25. Moses and the Red Sea

"Then Moses stretched out his hand over the sea, and the Lord drove the sea back by a strong east wind all night and made the sea dry land, and the waters were divided."
- Exodus 14:21

In the most spectacular event in the life of God's people, He proved His power and care for them. They were stuck with nowhere to turn. In front of them was the great Red Sea. There's no way they could safely cross with all the older men, women, and children. Behind them was Pharaoh's army. It seemed as if there was no way out for God's people.

But then God did what only God can do. He told Moses to take his staff and raise it above the sea. As he did that, God made the Sea to split apart. In a water walkway, God's people were able to go across dry land. Before Pharaoh's army could follow them through, He made the water come crashing back down. God had saved His people and was leading them to a Promised Land.

**Dear God, You are mighty to save.
I will trust in You for all of my life. Amen.**

26. Water From the Rock

"Behold, I will stand before you there on the rock at Horeb, and you shall strike the rock, and water shall come out of it, and the people will drink." And Moses did so, in the sight of the elders of Israel." - Exodus 17:6

Mere weeks after the crossing of the Red Sea, God's people had lost all faith and confidence in Him. They had started their journey into the wilderness and quickly ran out of food. Once their stomach started gurgling, they forgot how God had provided for them in the past. So they grumbled against God and Moses.

God, being ever so patient with them, provided for them again. In the middle of a dessert, God told Moses to go to a rock and take the same staff from the Red Sea. Using that staff, he would hit the rock, and God would make water come out of it. Once again, God's people rejoice in His provision but seem to fail to rejoice in Him.

Dear God, You are always faithful to provide for me every need. Amen.

27. Manna from Heaven

"Then the Lord said to Moses, "Behold, I am about to rain bread from heaven for you, and the people shall go out and gather a day's portion every day, that I may test them, whether they will walk in my law or not." - Exodus 16:4

Not only did God's people lack water, but they also lacked food. They were desperate and hungry, and they grumbled against God and Moses again. This time God provided in a way that would feed them for the 40 years that they wandered in the desert. He did something amazing. In the morning, instead of dew on the ground, God made manna appear on the ground. Manna was a flaky type of bread that they could gather and eat. It tasted like honey.

The rule was that they could only gather enough for each day. If they tried to save any, it would rot. They had to trust that God would provide exactly what they needed each day of the journey. This was a beautiful test of their faith and proof of His faithfulness. Jesus is like our manna. He is exactly what we need each day.

Dear God, I don't always trust You with all of my needs. Remind me of how You can provide. Amen.

28. Moses and the 10 Commandments

"You shall have no other gods before me." - Exodus 20:3

After God had already saved them from Pharaoh's army and provided food and water for them in the wilderness, God led them to a mountain. Once they got there, God told Moses to come up on the mountain so that they could talk with each other. As Moses made his way up the mountain, he saw a cloud of smoke and fire at the top. He went into that cloud and had the honor of speaking with God.

There God told him all the rules that they needed to follow. He summarized them in 10 Commandments. These rules told Moses and God's people how life worked best. It also explains how God wanted to be worshiped. Based on the grace that God had shown them already, He is telling them to trust His ways and keep His commands. That's how God treats us too. His grace in Jesus leads us to obey His commands.

Dear God, I want to trust and obey You alone. Give me strength to follow You. Amen.

29. Moses and the Golden Calf

"And the Lord said to Moses, "Go down, for your people, whom you brought up out of the land of Egypt, have corrupted themselves." - Exodus 32:7

While Moses was on the mountain, learning from God how He wanted to be worshiped, God's people had another plan in mind. They didn't want to wait for Moses to come back down and tell them what God said. They wanted to worship in their own way. So they looked around at the other nations to see what they were doing. They decided that they wanted to worship God by building a large golden calf. They were going to offer sacrifices to it.

God did not want them to do that. As He was telling Moses to not make any idols and to not worship any other gods, God's people were breaking those commands. So when Moses came down and saw the golden calf, he took the 10 Commandments that he had written on stone tablets and shattered them on the ground. This showed His people that they had already shattered God's rules. They were in trouble.

Dear God, I mess up like Your people did in the Bible. I like to do things my way instead of Your way. Thank You for always forgiving me. Amen.

30. Moses and the Tabernacle

God did not leave His people, even after their great disobedience. He took Moses back up the mountain and made new stone tablets with the 10 Commandments written on them. This showed His people that even though they will break His law, He will be there to restore them. The way this restoration would happen was through sacrifices at a tabernacle.

God gave them all the details they needed in order to build a mobile tabernacle. This would be a place they could set up and offer bulls, lambs, and goats as sacrifices for their sin. Both the tabernacle and the sacrifices are pictures of what Jesus did for us. He was a living tabernacle for God's people, and He became the sacrifice to pay for all sins on the cross.

Dear God, You are always ready and willing to forgive me when I ask. Amen.

31. Moses and the Fiery Serpents

"So Moses made a bronze serpent and set it on a pole. And if a serpent bit anyone, he would look at the bronze serpent and live." - Numbers 21:9

This probably won't surprise you very much at this point. God's people disobeyed again. They decided to follow their own ways instead of God's. And so, God punished them for their rebellion. He sent a brood of serpents into the camp. They were poisonous snakes that would kill you if they bit you. When the people saw this, they cried out to God for help. And, as always, God came to their rescue.

God told Moses to make a bronze serpent and raise it up on a stick. As long as the people kept their eyes on the bronze serpent, they would live, even if they were bitten. Like the bronze serpent, if we keep our eyes on Jesus, a man raised on the cross, we will find life.

Dear God, Your consistent love for Your people is awe-inspiring. Help me to keep my eyes on Jesus. Amen.

32. Moses and the 12 Spies

"Send men to spy out the land of Canaan, which I am giving to the people of Israel. From each tribe of their fathers you shall send a man, every one a chief among them." - Numbers 13:2

They made it. After years of traveling through the desert, surviving on water from rocks and manna from heaven, they finally made it to the Promised Land. As they stood on the edge of the river, looking out over the land they were to go into, they decided to send a few spies in. Spies are people that sneak in somewhere to find out what's going on. God's people decided to send in 12 spies to take a look around.

When the 12 spies got in, they saw that the land was full of fruit and cattle. They also saw that it was full of people. These people looked so big and strong; they called them giants. The spies ran back to God's people and said it was too risky. All except for 2 of them. Caleb and Joshua said they should trust God's promise. God's people did not follow Caleb and Joshua.

Dear God, it can be really hard to trust You when I've seen some scary things. Remind me of Your promises. Amen.

33. More Wandering

"For the people of Israel walked forty years in the wilderness, until all the nation, the men of war who came out of Egypt, perished, because they did not obey the voice of the Lord; the Lord swore to them that he would not let them see the land that the Lord had sworn to their fathers to give to us, a land flowing with milk and honey." - Joshua 5:6

As punishment for their disobedience and lack of faith, God said that His people could not enter the Promised Land for 40 years. That's a really long time! Over the next 40 years, they would have to wander around the desert, experiencing the thirst and hunger that they complained about so much beforehand. Instead of getting to enjoy the land flowing with milk and honey, they would be stuck with very little to live off of.

The punishment was long and severe, but it was not without reason. God wanted to teach them over that long period of time about His own faithfulness. You see, God would continue to provide for them. He would continue to send down the manna and have water flow from rocks if needed. Although it would be a difficult 40 years, they would learn more and more about God's grace.

Dear God, there are days that are really difficult. Help me to see what You're showing me about yourself in those days. Amen.

34. The Promise to Rahab

"And the men said to her, "Our life for yours even to death! If you do not tell this business of ours, then when the Lord gives us the land we will deal kindly and faithfully with you." "
- Joshua 2:14

Remember the 12 spies that went into the Promised Land? While they were there, they met a woman named Rahab. She hid them away from the soldiers that were looking for them. She saved their lives. In return, those spies promised to keep her and her family safe when God's people would come in and take over the city.

The time had finally come for God's people to go into the Promised Land and fight against those who were there. And God guided them and protected them all the way. And when they came to Rahab's home, they kept their promise and protected them. God's people were finally starting to act like Him. They were keeping promises. Jesus, being the very imprint of God's nature, kept His promises too. He said, "You will have trouble in this world, but take heart because I have overcome the world!"

Dear God, I want to be a promise keeper like You are. Let me be a person who keeps my word. Amen.

35. Battle of Jericho

"So the people shouted, and the trumpets were blown. As soon as the people heard the sound of the trumpet, the people shouted a great shout, and the wall fell down flat so that the people went up into the city, every man straight before him, and they captured the city." - Joshua 6:20

The first battle that God's people faced as they entered the Promised Land was the battle of Jericho. It seemed like an impossible situation. When they walked up to the city on a hill, all they could see was a massive wall. It was a wall so high they couldn't begin to climb it. It was a wall so long that it wrapped around the entire city. How could they possibly win the battle if they couldn't even get into the city?

When they failed to make a plan, God had a miraculous one in mind. He told them to march around the city silently once a day for a week. On the seventh day, He told them to march silently around the city seven times. After completing that last lap, He told them to make as much noise as possible. With screams of victory and trumpet blasts, the walls fell down flat. This was the beginning of the end of the battle.

Dear God, You always have a plan that will give You honor and praise. I want to trust that plan. Amen.

36. Deborah

"Now Deborah, a prophetess, the wife of Lappidoth, was judging Israel at that time."
- Judges 4:4

Battle after battle, God's people took over the Promised Land. Along the way, God went before them and fought on their behalf. He gave them victory after victory. After all the fighting was over, God's people began to settle in the Promised Land. But they still needed leadership from God. And so God raised up people called judges. These are not like the judges you might be thinking about. They didn't sit in a courtroom and make legal decisions. These judges did more than that. They helped make those big decisions, but they were also military leaders. Deborah is one of the first judges and the only female judge. She was a great example of what it meant to be a leader among God's people.

Dear God, You will never leave Your people without godly leadership. Thank You for the example of Deborah. Amen.

37. Gideon

"And Gideon said to him, "Please, my lord, if the Lord is with us, why then has all this happened to us? And where are all his wonderful deeds that our fathers recounted to us, saying, 'Did not the Lord bring us up from Egypt?' But now the Lord has forsaken us and given us into the hand of Midian." - Judges 6:13

Gideon was another one of the judges that God used to rescue His people. What happened during this time is God's people would stray from Him spiritually. They would start to worship other gods and follow their rules instead of His. He would discipline them by sending in an army from another nation to start a war against them. Then His people would cry out for help, and He would raise up a judge to save them.

This time, the nation that was attacking God's people was Mideon, and the judge God raised to save them was Gideon. To put it simply, Gideon was a scaredy-cat! He didn't want to be used by God to save His people. But God gave him the strength and courage to win the battles he faced.

Dear God, I admit that I am scared sometimes. Please give me strength and courage when I'm faced with hard things. Amen.

38. Samson's Strength

"For behold, you shall conceive and bear a son. No razor shall come upon his head, for the child shall be a Nazirite to God from the womb, and he shall begin to save Israel from the hand of the Philistines." - Judges 13:5

Perhaps the most significant judge in Israel's history is Samson. We have the most information on his life and how he sacrificed it for God's people in the end. Samson's story begins with a promise his mom made to God. She promised that she would raise him as a Nazarite. Basically, that means that she would not cut his hair or let him eat certain foods. God promised to give him strength in return.

God used Samson to win battle after battle against the Philistines. Although he made plenty of mistakes in his life, God was gracious and continued to supply all the physical strength he needed to lead the battles for God's people.

Dear God, You have a plan for my life that is based on a promise You've made. Teach me to follow that plan. Amen.

39. Samson's Sacrifice

"And Samson grasped the two middle pillars on which the house rested, and he leaned his weight against them, his right hand on the one and his left hand on the other."
- Judges 16:29

As I mentioned before, Samson made some pretty serious mistakes in his life. The worst one he made was when he told the secret of his strength to Delilah. As long as Samson did not cut his hair, God promised to continue to give him great physical strength. Samson told Delilah (one of the enemies of God's people), and she cut his hair while he was sleeping. The Philistine soldiers burst into the room and captured Samson.

Shortly after, Samson was chained in the middle of an auditorium. The Philistines laughed at him and humiliated him. Samson called out to God. And guess what God did. He let his hair start growing back again. This was a sign of grace to him. Then God gave Samson the strength to be able to pull down the pillars of the auditorium. He lost his life, but he took down all of the Philistines with him and saved God's people.

Dear God, You show grace to me when I least deserve it. Your compassion is amazing. Amen.

40. Ruth and Naomi

"But Ruth said, "Do not urge me to leave you or to return from following you. For where you go I will go, and where you lodge I will lodge. Your people shall be my people, and your God my God." - Ruth 1:16

The story of Ruth is a pure love story. It has a great love of a mother-in-law towards her daughter-in-law. There is a beautiful love between a widow and her new husband. It has a sovereign love story of God and His people. Let's think about that first love this time. Ruth was married to Naomi's son. However, her son passed away, and her husband did too.

Naomi decided to move back home to be close to her family, and she told Ruth that she should do the same. But Ruth and Naomi loved each other so much that Ruth said she wanted to stay with Naomi. She was so loved by Naomi that she committed to following the God that had made her that way. God would use that relationship to lead to the birth of King David's great grandfather.

Dear God, You are always working behind the scenes to bring about incredible endings to our stories. Amen.

"For this child, I prayed, and the Lord has granted me my petition that I made to him."
- 1 Samuel 1:27

After the time of the judges, God's people decided that they needed a king like all of the other nations. God reminded them that He was their King, but they continued to complain and beg for a king. So God warned them but made way for a king. The very beginning of that story starts with a woman who desperately wants to be a mom. She prays to God and asks for a son. She even promises that if God gives her a son, then she will commit him to the Lord.

God answered that prayer, and Hannah gave birth to a little baby boy named Samuel. God would use Samuel in a very important way to lead His people. God used Samuel to anoint the very first king of His people, Saul.

Dear God, I am so glad that You hear my prayers and that You will answer them. Amen.

42. Samuel is Called

"And the Lord came and stood, calling as at other times, "Samuel! Samuel!" And Samuel said, "Speak, for your servant hears." - 1 Samuel 3:10

The little baby boy grew up under the care of the priest named Eli. One night, while Samuel was lying in his bed, he heard someone calling for him. The voice called out, "Samuel! Samuel!" And so Samuel got up and ran to Eli's room to ask him what he wanted. But Eli said that he didn't call for him. This happened three times. On the third time, Eli had figured out what was going on.

He told Samuel to go back to bed. When the voice called out again, Eli told Samuel to answer it and say, "Speak, for your servant hears." So, Samuel did that, and the Lord spoke to him. Most of us won't have an experience like Samuel, where God speaks to us in the night. But if we have God's word, He speaks to us every time we read it.

Dear God, I am so thankful that You speak to me through Your word. Amen.

43. Saul Becomes King

"Then Samuel took a flask of oil and poured it on his head and kissed him and said, "Has not the Lord anointed you to be prince over his people Israel? And you shall reign over the people of the Lord and you will save them from the hand of their surrounding enemies. And this shall be the sign to you that the Lord has anointed you to be prince over his heritage." - Samuel 10:1

Remember when God's people begged God for a king, even though He was their King? Well, after warning them that it was a bad decision, God gave them a king. His name was Saul. God used Samuel when he grew up to anoint Saul as king. This means that Samuel did a special ceremony and poured oil over Saul's head to show that he had been chosen by God to lead His people.

Saul was a good king for a while. However, Saul was a jealous and prideful king in the end. He wanted all the glory for any of his victories in battle, even though it was God who had won the fights for him. Jesus is not like Saul. He is always a good King. Never jealous or prideful. He is humble and confident in His Father.

Dear God, You have given us a much better king than Saul. Thank you for King Jesus. Amen.

44. David Anointed as King

"And he sent and brought him in. Now he was ruddy and had beautiful eyes and was handsome. And the Lord said, "Arise, anoint him, for this is he." - 1 Samuel 16:12

While Saul was still king, God was preparing David to be the new king of Israel. God sent Samuel to a man named Jesse's house. He had plenty of sons that were strong and brave. Samuel met them all to determine which one was supposed to be the new king. He went down the line, and none of them were right. So he asked Jesse if there were any more sons he could meet.

Jesse said he had one more son that was young and small. He was out in the field shepherding the sheep. Jesse called that son in from the field. His name was David. When Samuel met David, God made it clear that he was supposed to be the next king of Israel. God wanted the next king to be more like a shepherd than a warrior.

Dear God, Your wisdom is greater than mine. You look past my body and see my heart. Amen.

45. David and Goliath

"Then David said to the Philistine, "You come to me with a sword and with a spear and with a javelin, but I come to you in the name of the Lord of hosts, the God of the armies of Israel, whom you have defied." - 1 Samuel 17:45

After being anointed as the new king, it was a while before David actually became the new king. During that time, while he was waiting, God continued to use and prepare David to be the king. There was another nation that was starting to pick a fight with God's people. They sent out their biggest and strongest warrior named Goliath. They told God's people to send their biggest and best.

All of God's people were too scared to try to fight Goliath, including king Saul. But David, when he heard about this, was not scared. He stepped up to fight Goliath. He didn't bring a sword or armor. He just brought a sling and a few smooth stones. With all of his confidence in God, he slung a stone and knocked Goliath out.

Dear God, I pray that You would give me confidence in You like David had. Amen.

46. David and Benjamin

*"Then Jonathan made a covenant with David,
because he loved him as his own soul."*
- 1 Samuel 18:3

David's victory over Goliath made him a very popular man. Everyone loved him and was excited that he would be the new king. Everyone except for king Saul. All of this caused Saul to hate David. He even tried to kill David. But David had a best friend who protected him. His name was Jonathan, Saul's son.

One time, when Saul was chasing David, Jonathan secretly told David to go one way and then told Saul that he had gone another way. Jonathan risked his own life and his relationship with his dad to protect David. Jesus, our greater friend, sacrificed His life so that we would have a relationship with His Father.

**Dear God, what a friend I have in Jesus!
Thank You for His love. Amen.**

47. Nathan calls out David

"Nathan said to David, "You are the man! Thus says the Lord, the God of Israel, 'I anointed you king over Israel, and I delivered you out of the hand of Saul." - 2 Samuel 12:7

While David was a great king, he wasn't perfect. In fact, he made one mistake that was horrible and wretched. He had a man killed in order to protect his own reputation. But he wasn't able to hide this sin from God. God sent a man named Nathan to confront David for his choices.

Nathan told David a story about a rich man who stole a poor man's lamb. David was enraged that someone would do such a horrible thing when he had plenty of his own. Nathan told David, "You are that man!" David had taken a man's wife and his life when he had plenty of both.

Dear God, You see all of my sins and will not let them go. Thank You for good friends who call me to repentance. Amen.

48. King David

"In times past, when Saul was king over us, it was you who led out and brought in Israel. And the Lord said to you, 'You shall be shepherd of my people Israel, and you shall be prince over Israel.' "- 2 Samuel 5:2

After many trials, threats, and dangers, David was finally crowned the king of God's people. He would become one of the greatest kings in their history. This is because of how God had described him. David was going to lead like a shepherd. He would be gentle, patient, protective, and watchful.

Even with this great description of king David, there is a greater King that he was merely pointing us towards. Jesus is our great shepherd. He not only leads gently and patiently but sacrificially. He gave up His life on the cross of Calvary to save us from our sin and the punishment of death that comes with it.

Dear God, I love You. The sacrifice of Your Son has saved my soul. Amen.

49. Psalm 23

"Even though I walk through the valley of the shadow of death, I will fear no evil, for you are with me; your rod and your staff, they comfort me." - Psalm 23:4

One of the incredible things about king David was that he was a musician. Even before taking the throne, you could find him playing his harp and singing songs. God used him to write some songs for the books of Psalms. Perhaps the most famous one of all of the songs of David is Psalm 23.

In it, David expresses his deep trust in God. Even in the 'valley of the shadow of death,' he is confident in God's love for him. He says that God's rod and staff bring him comfort. The rod was used to protect him, and the staff was used to lead him. God cares so deeply for His people and will not leave them alone.

Dear God, You promise me that You will never leave me nor forsake me. Amen.

50. The Wise King

"Give your servant therefore an understanding mind to govern your people, that I may discern between good and evil, for who is able to govern this your great people?"
- 1 Kings 3:9

David had a few sons, and one of them named Solomon became the next king of God's people. God asked Solomon what He could give Solomon. He thought about it and ultimately decided that if God gave him wisdom, he would be able to lead God's people well. This request made God glad. God made him the wisest man to ever live.

From Solomon, we have the Proverbs, which is a book of wise sayings. We also have the book of Ecclesiastes, which explains the meaning of life. And we have the Song of Solomon, which explains the love between a man and a woman. There was great wisdom shared with us in God's word because of how He blessed Solomon.

Dear God, the wisdom You have Solomon is still helping me today. Thank you. Amen.

51. God Watches Over Elijah

"He said, "I have been very jealous for the Lord, the God of hosts. For the people of Israel have forsaken your covenant, thrown down your altars, and killed your prophets with the sword, and I, even I only, am left, and they seek my life, to take it away." - 1 Kings 19:10

After Solomon, the kingdom of God's people began to fall apart. It split into two kingdoms and had a lot of really bad kings along the way. But God did not give up on His people. He continued to speak to them through prophets. One of those prophets was named Elijah.

Even after being used greatly by God, Elijah struggled with feeling alone. He would hide away in caves and by far away streams. He was convinced that God had left him alone with no one to partner with. But God provided food for him each time he ran away and constantly reassured him that he would never be alone.

Dear God, even if I don't feel Your presence, I can trust that You are near. Amen.

52. Elijah and the Widow

" The jar of flour was not spent, neither did the jug of oil become empty, according to the word of the Lord that he spoke by Elijah." - 1 Kings 17:16

Once while Elijah was traveling, he met a poor widow. He was so hungry and asked her for something to eat. Embarrassed by her situation, she barely had enough food for her and her son. She said that she couldn't spare anything at all. Elijah told her to trust God. He said that if she made him something to eat, God would not let her food run out.

As she prepared his food, the oil and flour that she used never ran out. In fact, it didn't run out for months after that. God honored her faith and provided for her. Can you imagine pouring oil out but never losing any? Or dipping a cup into the flour and never seeing a dent in it? Our God can provide everything we need.

Dear God, Your grace and miraculous love for me is astonishing. Amen.

53. Elijah on Mt Carmel

"And at the time of the offering of the oblation, Elijah the prophet came near and said, "O Lord, God of Abraham, Isaac, and Israel, let it be known this day that you are God in Israel, and that I am your servant, and that I have done all these things at your word." - 1 Kings 18:36

Elijah not only spoke to God's people, but he spoke to God's enemies too. He met a large group of men who followed a god named Baal. Elijah knew that his God was the only true God, and so he challenged them to a contest. He told them to build an altar on the top of the mountain and pray to their god. If he could light that altar on fire, then he would be the true God.

So the prophets of Baal prayed and jumped around and shouted. They begged their god to light the altar on fire. But nothing happened. Nothing would ever happen. So Elijah told his people to cover the altar in water and pour a mote of water around it to make it even harder on his God. Then prayed that God would send fire down from heaven. And His God did. Our God did.

Dear God, You are the one true God who has all power and might. I give You honor today. Amen.

54. Elijah Taken Away

"And as they still went on and talked, behold, chariots of fire and horses of fire separated the two of them. And Elijah went up by a whirlwind into heaven." - 2 Kings 2:11

Elijah was an incredible prophet for a lot of reasons, but one of the things that did not happen to any other prophets came at the end of his life. He and his successor, Elisha, were walking one day. They were talking about Elisha taking his place after he died and figuring out what that would look like. Little did Elisha know that Elijah was leaving that very day.

At the end of his time, Elijah was taken up into heaven by chariots of fire and horses of fire. In a whirlwind of glorious light, Elijah was gone. He did not experience death like Elisha would late, or like we will one day. He was picked up and placed directly into the presence of God.

Dear God, what an honor it must have been to be taken to heaven like that. I cannot wait to see You. Amen.

55. Jars of oil

"When the vessels were full, she said to her son, "Bring me another vessel." And he said to her, "There is not another." Then the oil stopped flowing. "- 2 Kings 4:6

Elijah's ministry as a prophet had ended, and Elisha's had started soon after. To show that Elisha was working for the same God, God allowed him to do a miracle that was like one of Elijah's. Elisha met a woman whose husband had died. She had a son to care for but no way to make any money. Elisha knew that she could sell her oil, but she only had a little bit.

Elisha told her to get as many empty jars from her neighbors as she could. She went out and collected a bunch. Then he told her to start filling them up from her little jar. An amazing thing happened as she started to pour. The little jar of oil never ran out. She was able to fill up so many jars until they were all full. Once again, God proved He can provide.

Dear God, I am so thankful that You can always provide for my needs. Amen.

56. Elisha Raises the Dead

"Then he went up and lay on the child, putting his mouth on his mouth, his eyes on his eyes, and his hands on his hands. And as he stretched himself upon him, the flesh of the child became warm." - 2 Kings 4:34

God did even greater things through Elisha than filling up some jars of oil. He even raised the dead back to life. This is what happened. A boy was helping his father in the field when all of a sudden, his head started to hurt. His father picked him up quickly and ran back to their house. But the little boy died shortly after.

They went to find Elisha because they knew that he knew God and had been used to do miracles in the past. Elisha prayed to God and laid on top of the little boy. When he did, the boy slowly came back to life. He sneezed seven times and then opened his eyes. God proved something amazing that day. He proved He had the power over life and death.

Dear God, there is no one else who can say that they have the power over life and death. You are amazing. Amen.

57. Naaman Healed

"So he went down and dipped himself seven times in the Jordan, according to the word of the man of God, and his flesh was restored like the flesh of a little child, and he was clean."
- 2 Kings 5:14

Naaman was a very powerful man. He was the commander of the Syrian army. They had just won a battle against God's people when he found out that he had leprosy. Leprosy is a disease that eats away at your skin and turns it white. Eventually, it will even fall off.
He lived at the same time that Elisha was alive. One of the little girls that was with God's people when Naaman attacked told him about Elisha. He went to Elisha for help, and Elisha told him to go and wash in the river seven times. That should not have cured Naaman, but God was at work. He healed him as he washed in the river. If God can heal His enemies, then He will surely heal us of our sins.

Dear God, You are gracious to all people, even your enemies. Help me to be the same. Amen.

58. The Boy King

"Josiah was eight years old when he began to reign, and he reigned thirty-one years in Jerusalem." - 2 Kings 22:1

God's people had a lot of different kings. Most of them were bad kings. But this king, king Josiah, was a really good king. What made him so special is that he became the king when he was eight years old. Can you imagine if the president was only eight years old? I'm surprised he didn't command everyone to make him macaroni and cheese all day long.

Josiah was special because of his age and because he found a very important book. One day he was exploring the old temple when he found an old dusty Bible. He had someone read it to him and tell him what it said. God spoke to him through the Bible, and Josiah led God's people to follow God again. God can do the same when we read His word.

Dear God, You can speak to me, even though I'm young. Please use Your word to tell me what I need to know. Amen.

59. The Brave Queen

"Then Esther spoke again to the king. She fell at his feet and wept and pleaded with him to avert the evil plan of Haman the Agagite and the plot that he had devised against the Jews." - Esther 8:3

God's people did not always have a good king. Sometimes, they didn't have a king at all. In fact, there were many times that the king they had was not one of God's people because they had been defeated in battle. This was one of those times. King Ahasuerus was an enemy king who was searching for a queen. He asked for all of the beautiful women to come and meet with him so he could pick the next queen.

One of the women he met was Esther. She was one of God's people. God used Esther's relationship with the enemy king to save His people. Because she was a good wife and queen, the king listened to her when God's people were in danger. God protected His people through Esther.

Dear God, You don't need a mighty king or warrior to accomplish Your plans. You can use anybody. Amen.

60. Fiery furnace

"He answered and said, "But I see four men unbound, walking in the midst of the fire, and they are not hurt; and the appearance of the fourth is like a son of the gods."
- Daniel 3:25

Another time when another enemy king ruled over God's people, there were three men named Shadrach, Meshach, and Abednego. They refused to bow down and worship the king's statue, and that got them into a lot of trouble. The punishment for not bowing down was being thrown into the fiery furnace. Even after being given a second chance, they would not bow down. The king had them thrown into the fire.

The furnace was so hot that the fire killed the soldiers that threw the three men in. But when the king looked into the furnace, he saw some men walking around. Not just three men, but four. The fourth man looked like a son of God. In fact, it was the Son of God, Jesus. He had saved them from the furnace, and that changed the king's heart.

Dear God, You are mighty to save Your people through Your Son. Give me faith in Him. Amen.

61. Daniel and the lion's den

"As he came near to the den where Daniel was, he cried out in a tone of anguish. The king declared to Daniel, "O Daniel, servant of the living God, has your God, whom you serve continually, been able to deliver you from the lions?" - Daniel 6:20

A new king came into power named Darius. He was also an enemy king. But he did not hate God's people. Darius had a really good friend named Daniel, who was one of God's prophets. But Darius' servants did not like Daniel. They wanted to be the only friends of the king, so they tricked Darius. They tricked him into signing a law that said they could only pray to him.

Daniel prayed to God every day. So when he was found praying to God, the soldiers took him and threw him into the lions' den. But an amazing thing happened. God shut the mouths of the lions and let Daniel survive a full day in the den. The next morning Darius ran out to the den, hoping that Daniel was still alive. God had saved him.

Dear God, You can use our friendships to show others about You. Let me be like that. Amen.

62. Jonah and the Big Fish

"And the Lord spoke to the fish, and it vomited Jonah out upon the dry land." - Jonah 2:10

Not all of God's prophets were strong and courageous men. Jonah was so scared of what God had asked him to do that he tried to run away. He got on a boat and tried to sail in the complete opposite direction of where God was telling him to go. But we cannot run away from God. God sent a big storm to the boat and threatened to sink it.

Jonah knew what was happening and told the sailors to toss him overboard. The moment he touched the water, the storm calmed. God could have let Jonah drown. He was being rebellious. But God loves His people, even when they seem unlovable. God sent a big fish to swallow Jonah and carry him back to dry land.

Dear God, I know that I act unlovable sometimes. Thank You for always loving me. Amen.

63. Angel and Mary

"And behold, you will conceive in your womb and bear a son, and you shall call his name Jesus." - Luke 1:31

God's people kept rebelling against Him and turning their backs to Him. Eventually, God stopped sending prophets. For years and years, there was nothing but silence from God. It felt like God had left His people alone. He was supposed to be sending a Savior that would save His people forever. But where was He now? Had He finally given up on His people?

While God's people were wondering this, an angel appeared to a woman who lived in Nazareth called Mary. It was the first time that God had spoken to His people in hundreds of years. That angel told Mary to get ready because she was going to have a baby. His name would be Jesus, and He would save God's people.

Dear God, You promise that You will never leave me or forsake me. Thank You for sending Your Son to save me. Amen.

64. Angel and Joseph

"But as he considered these things, behold, an angel of the Lord appeared to him in a dream, saying, "Joseph, son of David, do not fear to take Mary as your wife, for that which is conceived in her is from the Holy Spirit." - Matthew 1:20

To help Mary believe what she had been told and to help others believe too, God sent an angel to Joseph, Mary's soon-to-be husband. He made sure to tell Joseph separately from Mary. That way, when they got together later to share the good news with each other, they would be able to believe each other. You have to admit, having the Son of God is a hard story to believe.

Joseph even had a hard time believing it at first. But God helped him to see and understand what was happening. Joseph had been chosen for this very special task, to raise Jesus as his own son. Joseph trusted God and Mary. Together they got ready to have Jesus as their son.

Dear God, it can be hard to believe Your message sometimes. Use Your Spirit to teach me what is true. Amen.

65. Jesus is Born

"And she gave birth to her firstborn son and wrapped him in swaddling clothes and laid him in a manger, because there was no place for them in the inn." - Luke 2:7

The greatest moment in history had finally come. Not only did God end His silence among His people, He decided that He would send His only Son to live among His people. He sent Him as a baby boy. When he was born, it was not in the comfort of a hospital or even a home. They were traveling for a census. They didn't even get to stay in a hotel.

Jesus was born in a stable behind the inn. There wasn't a bed for baby Jesus, so they laid him down in a manger. A manger is what animals ate their food out of. The Son of God, deserving all honor and praise, was born in a barn and laid in a trough. What was God up to? Wasn't He supposed to be sending a king or a warrior to save His people?

Dear God, Your plans do not always make sense to me. Help me to trust Your heart. Amen.

66. Shepherds Visit

"For unto you is born this day in the city of David a Savior, who is Christ the Lord."
- Luke 2:11

King Jesus had been born. Although His birth was not what God's people expected, surely the first people to find out about this great birth would have been important people. Maybe God was going to tell the king to move over and make room. Maybe God was going to find a prophet to tell. No, God decided to tell shepherds. Stinky shepherds who were working in their field at night.

While they were watching their sheep, an angel appeared to them and told them the great news that Jesus had been born. At first, they were really scared. You would be too. But then they were really excited and ran off to find this baby. The angel told them where to look: in a stable. They probably knew just the one.

Dear God, Your Son was born in a manger and greeted by shepherds. I know You are up to something big. Amen.

67. Simeon's Promise

"And it had been revealed to him by the Holy Spirit that he would not see death before he had seen the Lord's Christ."
- Luke 2:26

The next person to meet baby Jesus is more of what you would expect. There was a man named Simeon who was a priest in the temple. It was traditional for one of God's people to be circumcised by a priest when they were eight days old. So, when Jesus turned eight days old, Joseph and Mary brought Him to the temple.

What they didn't know was the promise that God made Simeon. A long time ago, God promised Simeon that he would not die until he had seen the Savior of God's people. Then it finally happened. Simeon knew it the moment he held Jesus in his hands. God was fulfilling promises to His people individually and as a whole.

Dear God, You make sweet promises to me, and You keep each one. Amen.

68. Wise Men Visit

"And going into the house, they saw the child with Mary his mother, and they fell down and worshiped him. Then, opening their treasures, they offered him gifts, gold and frankincense and myrrh." - Matthew 2:11

Word had started to spread about baby Jesus being born. People from all over were talking about this new baby who was the Promised King and Savior of God's people. This made everyone so excited. Well, almost everyone. You see, God's people already had a king named Herod. He did not want to give up his throne. So he tricked some wise men. He told them to go and find the new King so he could worship him.

The wise men went. They followed a star that stayed over Jesus' home. When they found him, they treated Him like a king. They offered Him wonderful presents, even though He was only two years old. God warned the wise men after their visit that Herod was lying. They told Jesus His family to run away and hide.

Dear God, Your plans cannot be stopped, even by powerful kings. That gives me hope. Amen.

69. King Herod's Anger

"Then Herod, when he saw that he had been tricked by the wise men, became furious, and he sent and killed all the male children in Bethlehem and in all that region who were two years old or under, according to the time that he had ascertained from the wise men." - Matthew 2:16

King Herod was furious that the wise men had saved Jesus and his family from the king. He was so mad that he made a horrible rule. It was a rule that reminded God's people of being back in Egypt under the wicked Pharaoh. He made a rule that said all of the male children in Bethlehem that were around Jesus' age had to be killed.

Herod was hoping to get Jesus killed with this rule. But all he did was get a bunch of his own people killed and make everyone mad at him. Ironically, It was safer in Egypt for Jesus than it was among His own people. But just like with Moses, Jesus would come out of Egypt to save God's people.

Dear God, I am sad when I hear about such wickedness in people. Keep me from growing so cold to You. Amen.

70. Young Jesus is Lost

"After three days they found him in the temple, sitting among the teachers, listening to them and asking them questions." - Luke 2:46

Jesus grew up just like you, and I do. He had to eat His fruits and vegetables, listen to His Mom and Dad, and even go to school. One time, when they were on their way home from a festival, Jesus went to the temple to learn more about God. His parents didn't know that's where He went. They thought He was with an aunt or an uncle. So they headed home without Him.

It took them three days to find Him. When they finally did, they found Him in the temple, learning and asking questions. Jesus was confused on why they couldn't find Him. He knew that He was supposed to be doing whatever God had told Him to do, so naturally, He would be spending time at the temple.

Dear God, sometimes I want to look for You in all of the wrong places. Remind me that I can always find Your will in Your word. Amen.

71. Jesus' Baptism

"And when Jesus was baptized, immediately he went up from the water, and behold, the heavens were opened to him, and he saw the Spirit of God descending like a dove and coming to rest on him." - Matthew 3:16

When Jesus was around thirty years old, it was time for Him to start His ministry. It was time for Him to start traveling to preach the gospel, heal the sick, and help the poor. To begin His ministry, He wanted to be an example to anyone who would believe in Him. He needed to be baptized. Baptism is a physical sign of an inward change.

When a person is baptized, they are laid down in the water and raised back up. This is supposed to represent our old way of life being laid down to death and our new life in Jesus coming forth. When Jesus did this, God confirmed who He was in front of everyone. He said, "This is my beloved Son, with whom I am well pleased."

Dear God, the sign of baptism is a precious gift. Show me when I need to be baptized. Amen.

72. Jesus Chooses Disciples

Once Jesus started His ministry, He didn't want to do it alone. He knew that He could accomplish more if He had a team of people to work with. So Jesus went to twelve men and asked them to follow Him. Those men were called His disciples. This just means that they agreed to travel with Him, learn about God from Him, and try to live as He lived.

Don't miss this amazing fact. Jesus did not need help. He wanted to include people in the work He was doing, but He didn't need the help. Think about it. Jesus is God. He could do anything He wanted without even breaking a sweat. But Jesus loves His people and wants to have a relationship with them. So He calls us to follow Him.

Dear God, You have asked me to follow Your Son. I want to do that. Amen.

73. First Miracle

"This, the first of his signs, Jesus did at Cana in Galilee, and manifested his glory. And his disciples believed in him."
- John 2:11

Jesus did a lot of miracles during His life. So many, in fact that the disciple John said that if all of them were written down, the world could not contain all of the books. The miracles began at a friend's wedding in Cana. The wedding reception was mid-swing, but all of the wine was gone. The party hosts knew that this problem would end the celebration too early.

They brought the problem to Jesus. He turned the water jars into wine. This is amazing because it takes years to make good wine, and Jesus did it in seconds. The party continued on. Jesus didn't do this just because He wanted the party to continue. He did it to prove that He truly was God's Son, able to do the impossible.

Dear God, You care about Your people, even the simple problems they face. Amen.

74. The Demon-Possessed Man

Jesus was able to do far more than turn water into wine. He was able to handle any physical problem that people faced as well as the spiritual issues. One of the more severe circumstances that Jesus came across was with a demon-possessed man. He was so miserable and desperate that he was living in a graveyard. All the people who loved him no longer recognized him anymore.

But Jesus knew who he was. He went up to him and spoke directly to the demon that had possessed his body. The demon trembled before Jesus and begged him to send them away instead of destroying them. So Jesus sent them into a herd of pigs, and they ran away.

Dear God, You are so strong that the demons tremble before You. Amen.

"He said to him, 'If they do not hear Moses and the Prophets, neither will they be convinced if someone should rise from the dead.'" - Luke 18:31

Jesus was not just a miracle worker but a master teacher. The way that He taught His disciples and the crowds that would come and go was through parables. Parables are earthly stories with heavenly meanings. Jesus loved to tell stories in order to teach a lesson about God.

One time He told a story about a rich man and a beggar named Lazarus. Both of these men died, and they went to two different places. The rich man was separated from God, and Lazarus was united with God. The rich man was so miserable that he begged for even a drop of water from Lazarus' finger. But the separation between God and the rich man was too great.

Dear God, one day I will be united with You forever. Give me a desire to tell others about You. Amen.

76. Persistent Prayer

*"Yet because this widow keeps bothering me,
I will give her justice, so that she will not beat me
down by her continual coming." - Luke 18:5*

Another parable that Jesus told was about an annoying old woman. No, seriously. He told a story about a widowed woman who lived near a judge in the city. She needed his help but couldn't get it. So she went to his house every night and knocked on his door. If he didn't answer, she called out at his window all night until he answered. Eventually, the judge gave up and helped her.

The point was that if a judge who is annoyed with someone will send help, how much more would God, who loves His people, help them when they call. He doesn't find us annoying and ignore us. He knows what we need and is waiting to give it to us.

Dear God, I am thankful that You don't find my prayers annoying. You love to hear from me.
Amen.

"Other seeds fell on good soil and produced grain, some a hundredfold, some sixty, some thirty." - Matthew 13:8

Some of the parables that Jesus told were funny stories. Some were sad stories. And some were strange stories that were hard to understand. When Jesus saw that the disciples were confused about the story He was telling them, He explained it to them again in another way. Like I said before, Jesus was a master teacher.

The parable of the different stories tells us about how different people hear God's word. Some are like good soil that receive the seeds of God's word and let them grow. Other people are like thorny soil. With them, God's word gets overcrowded by the thorns of anxiety and stress. What kind of soil are you like?

Dear God, I pray that You would make me into a good soil that loves Your word. Amen.

78. Parable of the Talents

"To one he gave five talents, to another two, to another one, to each according to his ability. Then he went away."
- Matthew 25:15

Jesus told another story about being a good servant. The ears of the disciples perked up with this one because they were all trying to be a servant like Jesus was. Jesus told a story about a man who was going away on a long journey, and he gave his servants some money.
One of the servants put the money in the bank and kept it safe. One of them invested the money and made more money with it. The last servant dug a hole and buried it in the ground. When the man came back from the trip, he was upset with the last servant. He didn't use the gift that he gave him. He hid it away. A good servant uses the gift that the master gives to serve him.

Dear God, I want to be a good servant that uses the gifts You give me. Amen.

"Then his master summoned him and said to him, 'You wicked servant! I forgave you all that debt because you pleaded with me." - Matthew 18:32

This next parable might make you mad. You'll be so offended by what the servant did. Let me tell you about it. There was a servant who was in deep debt. He had borrowed a lot of money from his master, and he wasn't able to pay him back. He made up excuses for why he couldn't pay the master back and even hid from him. One day, enough was enough, and the master caught him.

But instead of punishing him, he forgave his debt. He said that the servant didn't owe him anymore. That was great news. But guess what the servant did after that. On his way home, he caught a guy who owed him a few bucks. The guy couldn't pay him, so he threw him in jail. How could he refuse to forgive this small debt when he was forgiven such a big one?

Dear God, help me to always remember that You have forgiven me so much so I can forgive others. Amen.

80. Parable of Mustard Seed

"It is the smallest of all seeds, but when it has grown it is larger than all the garden plants and becomes a tree, so that the birds of the air come and make nests in its branches." - Matthew 13:32

Some of the parables that Jesus told were long stories. A few were just one or two sentences long. The parable of the mustard seed was a really short one. So short, I'll just quote it here for you. He said, "The kingdom of heaven is like a grain of mustard seed that a man took and sowed in his field."

The point of this parable is to tell how the kingdom of God will grow. It starts out tiny, like a mustard seed. But when it grows, it grows into an enormous tree that is hard to even believe. God's kingdom will be like that. It will start with just Jesus, but it will be full of people in the end.

**Dear God, I see You growing Your kingdom.
I want to help. Amen.**

81. Parable of Hidden Treasure

"The kingdom of heaven is like treasure hidden in a field, which a man found and covered up. Then in his joy he goes and sells all that he has and buys that field."
- Matthew 13:44

The last parable we are going to learn about is one of the shortest ones. It simply says that a man found treasure in a field one day. He buried the treasure in the ground and went to go buy the field. He did this so that he could have the treasure rightfully as his own.

The meaning of this parable is just as simple. Jesus is the greatest treasure in the world. With Him, we have a relationship with God that is safe and life-giving. We should be so excited about this relationship that we will treat Him like a treasure.

Dear God, help me to treasure you like the man in the parable. Amen.

82. Counting the Cost

"For which of you, desiring to build a tower, does not first sit down and count the cost, whether he has enough to complete it?" - Luke 14:28

It costs a lot to follow Jesus. It doesn't cost a lot of money. Jesus didn't have a lot of money either. But it costs following Him no matter what. Not everyone liked Jesus. Some people even hated Him. If we want to be His disciple, we must be willing to follow Him, even if it means being hated for it.

Jesus says that before we choose to follow Him, we need to count the cost. We need to think about what trouble may come for us if we decide to follow Him. If we think He is worth the price, then we will be able to follow Him through it all. Trust me, friend. Jesus is worth every cost that may come your way.

Dear God, Show me what it will cost to follow You. And then show me that You're worth it. Amen.

83. Sermon on the Mount

" Seeing the crowds, he went up on the mountain, and when he sat down, his disciples came to him." - Matthew 5:1

Jesus was a miracle worker, a storyteller, and a preacher. His longest recorded sermon is called the sermon on the mount. This wasn't a very clever name. Jesus literally just preached a sermon on the side of a mountain, and the name just kind of stuck. This was a very important sermon for Jesus to preach because it made it really clear what He came to do.

He came to fulfill the law and offer salvation through following Him and not following the law. He wasn't saying that the law wasn't important. He was just explaining that He saves, not the law. He even says that we cannot keep the law unless we've been saved by Him, to begin with. This changed everything.

**Dear God, teach me over and over again
that I am saved by Jesus alone. Amen.**

84. Building on The Rock

"And the rain fell, and the floods came, and the winds blew and beat on that house, but it did not fall, because it had been founded on the rock." - Matthew 7:25

At the end of His sermon, Jesus taught that if you followed what He said, you would be like a man building a house. If you followed Jesus, you would build your house on a rock. This house could withstand any hurricane or flood that came up against it.

He, then, said that if we didn't listen to Him, we would be like a man building a house on sand. What happens to a sandcastle when the waves crash over it? It crumbles bit by bit each time. When we try to follow other gods or think that there is no god at all, our lives will wash away bit by bit.

Dear God, I want to build my life on the rock of Your Son, Jesus. Amen.

85. Sheep from Goats

"Then he will say to those on his left, 'Depart from me, you cursed, into the eternal fire prepared for the devil and his angels.'" - Matthew 25:41

Some of the things that Jesus taught His disciples were pretty scary. This is the kind of thing that we find in the story about the sheep and the goats. He says that one day, He will judge all people. He will examine their hearts and their lives and put them into two groups. To His right, He will be those who are His sheep as He is the Good Shepherd. On the His left, He will put the goats.

The goats will be sent away from Him forever. Jesus didn't leave us to guess what the goats and the sheep look like. He told us how their hearts worked. The sheep cared for the least of these. This means that they did all they could for those who were in need.

Dear God, give me a heart like a sheep.
I want to do all I can for others. Amen.

86. The Lord's Prayer

"Our Father in heaven, hallowed be your name. Your kingdom come, your will be done, on earth as it is in heaven. Give us this day our daily bread, and forgive us our debts, as we also have forgiven our debtors. And lead us not into temptation, but deliver us from evil."
- Matthew 6:9-13

If you have ever wondered how to pray or wanted to be a better person of prayer, then you need to spend time thinking about this passage of Scripture. That's exactly what Jesus talked about here because the disciples had asked Him how to pray.

This is not a magic prayer that has special powers and can sway God one way or another. It's an example prayer for us to follow. It tells us to honor God when we pray. It tells us to pray for His will. It tells us to ask to be used by God and to be forgiven by Him. It tells us to pray for spiritual protection in our lives. Pray this way.

Dear God, I want to pray more faithfully.
Teach me to pray like Jesus. Amen.

87. The Centurion's Faith

"And to the centurion Jesus said, "Go; let it be done for you as you have believed." And the servant was healed at that very moment." - Matthew 8:13

A powerful soldier, called a centurion, was desperate. So desperate that he came to Jesus for help. This was a surprising thing because this soldier was supposed to hate Jesus. He was supposed to be trying to stop Jesus' ministry, not adding to it. But this centurion knew that Jesus was his only hope. He had faith that Jesus could heal his servant.

Jesus saw into the heart of the centurion and saw His faith. He was glad to see it and was more than willing to heal the servant of the centurion. In fact, before the centurion could even make it back to his house, the servant was already healed.

Dear God, You delight to see faith in me. Give me the faith I need. Amen.

88. Hole in the Roof

More and more people were finding out about this amazing Jesus. He had done so many miracles, taught about God in profound ways, and made deep relationships with those around Him. Everyone was coming to meet him. One time there was a group of friends who had a paralyzed friend. This means that he couldn't move at all.

They wanted Jesus to heal their friend, and so they carried him to this house where Jesus was. But it was so crowded that they couldn't get in. So they did something crazy. They climbed onto the top of the house and dug a hole right through the roof. Then they lowered their friend down. Jesus, seeing their faith, healed their friend.

Dear God, Help me to be like this man's friend.
I want to do all I can, even crazy things,
to bring my friends to You. Amen.

"And he said to them, "Why are you afraid, O you of little faith?" Then he rose and rebuked the winds and the sea, and there was a great calm." - Matthew 8:26

Even though the disciples had been there for every miracle and heard all of the incredible teachings of Jesus, they still struggled with their faith. They struggled to trust Jesus with everything in their lives. One time, when they were sailing across the ocean, a great storm came. The storm was so strong that it scared even the most experienced sailors on the boat. But it didn't scare Jesus.

Jesus fell asleep in the middle of the storm. Can you believe that? He only woke up because the disciples were screaming in fear. Jesus got up and spoke a word. The wind and the waves obeyed His voice and grew calm. The disciples still had to learn that trusting Jesus meant trusting Him in the good times and the scary times.

Dear God, I want to be able to trust You, even in the stormy times in my life. Amen.

90. Full fishing net

"And Simon answered, "Master, we toiled all night and took nothing! But at your word I will let down the nets."
- Luke 5:5

One of Jesus' disciples was a man named Peter. Peter was a fisherman and a very good one at that. So when Jesus did this miracle, it meant something powerful for him. You see, Peter had been fishing all night long and hadn't caught a single fish. After the failed fishing trip, Peter and his friends were coming back to shore. There they found Jesus.

As they were pulling back in, Jesus told them to cast their nets on the other side of the boat. He said to give it one more try. Peter was exhausted but figured it couldn't hurt. So they cast their net on the other side of the boat. When they tried to pull it in, the net started to break because it was so full of fish. Through this experience, Jesus' ministry made sense to Peter. So he followed Jesus.

Dear God, I am thankful that You speak to me in a way that is meaningful to me. Amen.

91. Feed the 5000

"And they all ate and were satisfied. And they took up twelve baskets full of the broken pieces left over."
- Matthew 14:20

As the crowds of people grew that came to hear Jesus teach, it became the disciples' job to handle some of the practical details. One of those details was figuring out what everyone would eat. A good host provides the food for the people who come, but there were thousands. The bible says there were 5,000 men. So if you count their wives and children, there would have been at least 10,000 people there. And there were only 12 disciples with no money and no food.

Jesus was not anxious over this problem. He called out to a little boy who had his lunch with him. He asked to borrow it. Then He blessed it and began to give it away. With each piece He broke off, it never ran out. He and the disciples were able to satisfy everyone's hunger, all 10,000 people, with one boy's lunch.

Dear God, Nothing will stop You from providing for me. You can use the smallest lunch to feed me. Amen.

92. Walks on Water

"But when the disciples saw him walking on the sea, they were terrified, and said, "It is a ghost!" and they cried out in fear." - Matthew 14:26

Another storm had come while Jesus' disciples were sailing on the sea. However, this time Jesus was not with them. He had gone away for a little while to pray and spend some time with Himself. While the storm was raging on, they saw something on the water. As their eyes cleared, they saw that it was a person and it looked like a ghost. They were terrified. But it wasn't their demise. It was their savior standing there.

Jesus was walking on water, coming to their rescue. Jesus did not have to be in the boat to be their comfort. He didn't even have to be there when the storm started. He knew exactly where they were and what was going on. He showed up at exactly the right moment like He always does.

Dear God, if You're able to walk on water to save Your people, I have nothing to fear. Amen.

93. Heals the Blind Beggar

There was a blind man who sat at the gate to the city every day. He couldn't do anything else. He had to sit there and beg. There weren't any jobs for blind men back then. There wasn't any technology to help them or dogs to guide. So all they could do was sit and beg. When Jesus passed by, the blind man called out and asked for help.

The blind man didn't ask Jesus for the same thing he asked everyone else for. He normally asked for money, but he knew Jesus was able to help him in a greater way. He asked Jesus to give him his sight. And Jesus did.

Dear God, when I pray to You, I can ask for the impossible because You're able. Amen.

94. Money in fish

"However, not to give offense to them, go to the sea and cast a hook and take the first fish that comes up, and when you open its mouth you will find a shekel. Take that and give it to them for me and for yourself." - Matthew 17:27

Not everyone liked Jesus. Yes, He could do miracles, but He was always teaching too. Some people did not agree with what Jesus was teaching. They tried to think of different ways to get Him into trouble so He would have to stop.

One way they tried to get Him in trouble was by lying and saying that He wasn't paying His taxes like He ought to. Jesus showed that He was paying and was able to pay at any time by telling Peter to do something crazy. He said to go fishing, and you'll catch a fish with a coin in its mouth. Use that to pay the taxes.

Dear God, Your Son lived a perfect life, all the way down to how He respected the government. I trust in that perfection. Amen.

95. Good Samaritan

"He said, "The one who showed him mercy." And Jesus said to him, "You go, and do likewise." "- Luke 10:37

There was a man who was walking down a busy road one day. While he was reading home, the man was beaten and robbed on that road. He laid there, nearly dead, as men and women passed him by. There were two different religious leaders, men like pastors, who went to the other side of the road just to avoid him. But there was one man who stopped to help him. Jesus said he was a Samaritan.

To you, this may sound like a sweet story about kindness. But Jesus was telling this story to religious leaders who hated Samaritans. So when the Samaritan was the hero of the story, they were deeply offended. Jesus was making a point. It didn't matter if you were a religious leader or not; kindness is what Jesus wants from us.

Dear God, I want to be kind like the Good Samaritan. Give me opportunities to be. Amen.

96. Mary and Martha

"But the Lord answered her, "Martha, Martha, you are anxious and troubled about many things, but one thing is necessary. Mary has chosen the good portion, which will not be taken away from her." - Luke 10:41-42

Mary and Martha were two good friends of Jesus. He was over at their house one day for lunch and to spend time with them. While He was there, Martha was doing everything she could to be a good hostess. She was washing the dishes, setting the table, preparing the lunch, and everything else. She was doing this all by herself, but she wasn't happy about it.

Martha thought that Mary should have been helping her. Mary was just sitting down with Jesus, talking with Him while Martha worked. She tried to fuss at Mary, but Jesus stopped her. He said that Martha was too focused on secondary things. Mary was focused on the more important thing, Him.

Dear God, Help me to stay focused on the most important thing in my life, You. Amen.

97. Lost Sheep

"What man of you, having a hundred sheep, if he has lost one of them, does not leave the ninety-nine in the open country, and go after the one that is lost, until he finds it?"
- Luke 15:4

There was one lesson that was so important to Jesus that He taught it multiple times. In fact, He taught the same lesson, back-to-back-to-back. He taught the same lesson in three different ways to make sure that it stuck. These stories were the parables of the lost sheep, the lost coin, and the lost son.

In the parable of the lost sheep, Jesus tells about a shepherd who lost one of his 100 sheep. That shepherd was willing to leave the 99 sheep in order to look for the one lost sheep. The point of this parable and the following ones is to tell us that God loves us so much to come to find us when we are lost.

Dear God, I am so thankful that You will always come to find me when I'm lost. Amen.

98. Lost Coin

"Or what woman, having ten silver coins, if she loses one coin, does not light a lamp and sweep the house and seek diligently until she finds it?" - Luke 15:8

This next parable seems silly in light of the lost sheep. He tells about a woman who lost a coin. Let's say that that coin is a quarter. Not very valuable. He says that when this woman lost that coin that she searched the whole house for it. She was flipping over couch cushions and emptying out drawers to find it.

The crazy part is when she found it, she threw a party and invited all of her friends over. No doubt, this party cost her more than a quarter to throw. The point was this: she looked for the coin because it was valuable to her, even if others didn't think it was valuable. God comes to find us because we are valuable to Him.

Dear God, I question whether or not I am worth anything to anyone. Remind me that I am valuable to You. Amen.

99. Lost Son

"And he arose and came to his father. But while he was still a long way off, his father saw him and felt compassion, and ran and embraced him and kissed him." - Luke 15:20

In the final of the three parables, Jesus tells a story about a lost son. This time, the son is not lost like the coin or the sheep. The father of the son knows where he is. But the son has lost his way in life. He is making bad decisions and not following what his father had told him. When the son had wasted all of his money and found himself envying pigs and their slop, he decided to go home. He was ready to be found.

As he came over the hill, reciting his plea for forgiveness in his head, the father saw him. The father had been waiting for him to come home and watched for him every day. The moment the father saw his son, he ran out to greet him. He hugged him and dressed him, and reminded him that he will always be his son, no matter what.

Dear God, I am prone to losing my way in life. I praise You because You are always looking for me. Amen.

100. Ten Lepers

"Was no one found to return and give praise to God except this foreigner?" - Luke 17:18

Jesus did some incredible things for a bunch of people. Some of those people took advantage of Jesus' kindness and gave him no thanks or respect for the miracles He did for them. One time, there was a group of ten lepers that needed healing. Remember that leprosy was a skin disease that would slowly kill your skin. Because of this, these people were outcasts in their town and weren't allowed to be around other people. But Jesus came close to them.

Jesus healed all ten of those lepers, and that gave them the ability to go back to the city and rejoin their families. Only one of those men thanked Jesus. Only one. Jesus didn't heal these men for thanksgiving, but it is a good and right response to kindness to be thankful. We need to work hard to be thankful for all things.

Dear God, I pray that You will forgive me when I am not thankful for all that You do for me. Amen.

101. Jesus and the Children

"But when Jesus saw it, he was indignant and said to them, "Let the children come to me; do not hinder them, for to such belongs the kingdom of God." - Mark 10:14

Jesus loves everyone. The rich and the poor. The people that looked like Him and those that didn't. The old and the young. He loved them all. And so, when the children tried to run up to Him, He didn't turn them away. He wasn't too busy to spend time with them or too important to only talk to grown-ups.

Jesus even said that the kingdom of God belongs to people with child-like faith. This means that the only way to be with God in His kingdom forever was to have pure faith in Jesus without doubt. Do you have this kind of faith?

Dear God, I want to have child-like faith. I know You're trustworthy and love me. Amen.

102. Zaccheus

"And when Jesus came to the place, he looked up and said to him, "Zacchaeus, hurry and come down, for I must stay at your house today." Luke 19:5

Another example of how Jesus loves everyone is in the story about Zacchaeus. Nobody liked Zacchaeus because he was a dishonest man. He was a tax collector that used his power to take money from people. He was rich. But he was rich because of how he took advantage of other people. But Jesus still loved him.

Jesus loved him so much that He found Zacchaeus in a crowd and invited him to have lunch with him. The other people saw Jesus do that, and they were so confused. Didn't Jesus know how dishonest this man was? Jesus knew. He knows how sinful our hearts are too. And yet He still loves us. He wants to be with us.

Dear God, I am thankful that You did not overlook Zacchaeus. In a crowded place, You searched for Him. Amen.

103. Alabaster Jar

"A woman came up to him with an alabaster flask of very expensive ointment, and she poured it on his head as he reclined at table." - Matthew 26:7

Because Jesus loved everybody, all kinds of people showed their love for Him. There was a woman who loved Jesus so much that she wanted to give Him as much respect as she could. So she took her most expensive bottle of perfume and poured it on His head. This perfume cost so much money, so this was an incredible sacrifice for her.

The disciples didn't understand why she did that. They saw it as a waste of money. But Jesus knew what she was doing. She was trying to show her love in the best way she knew how. What can you do to show your love to Jesus today?

Dear God, sometimes saying I love You doesn't feel like enough. I want to show my love for You. Amen.

104. Lazarus raised

"When he had said these things, he cried out with a loud voice, "Lazarus, come out." The man who had died came out, his hands and feet bound with linen strips, and his face wrapped with a cloth. Jesus said to them, "Unbind him, and let him go." - John 11:43-44

Remember Mary and Martha, Jesus' friends? They had a brother named Lazarus, who was also a really good friend to Jesus. A tragic thing happened to Lazarus. He got really sick. So sick that he died. Jesus was out of town when this all happened. When Jesus was able to get back to town, he went to Mary and Martha's house. They were devastated and confused. How could Jesus heal everyone else, but not Lazarus?

Jesus wept over his friend, Lazarus. But He was not without hope. Jesus planned to bring him back to life before he ever died. And so, Jesus prayed to God and called out to Lazarus in the tomb. When he told Lazarus to come out, he came out. The dead man was now alive.

Dear God, You can raise the dead to life.
Only You can do that. Amen.

105. Triumphant Entry

"And those who went before and those who followed were shouting, "Hosanna! Blessed is he who comes in the name of the Lord! "- Mark 11:9

Jesus' ministry did not end how everyone expected. You see, a lot of people were following Jesus because they thought that He was going to be their new king. God's people were under Roman rule, and they thought Jesus was going to liberate them from that. So when Jesus was coming to Jerusalem to celebrate the Passover with God's people, they treated Him like a king.

They laid out palm branches as He rode into town on a donkey. They cried out, "Hosanna! Blessed is he who comes in the name of the Lord!" as He passed by. They were giving Him a royal welcome. While Jesus is a king coming to free His people, it wasn't from Roman rule. It was from the chains of sin and death.

Dear God, Your Son is the rightful King who can save me from my sins. Amen.

106. Widow's Mite

"And he said, "Truly, I tell you, this poor widow has put in more than all of them." - Luke 21:3

After riding into Jerusalem, Jesus made His way to the temple. When He arrived, He saw something interesting happen. There was a group of rich men who had lined up to loudly place their money into the offering box. They did it in such a way that they drew attention to themselves.

But there was also a poor widowed woman. She only had two copper coins. She gave both of them to the Lord. Everything she had, as little as it was, she gave to Him. Jesus saw this action and said that she had given more than any of the rich men. It wasn't more money, but it definitely cost her more. It required actual faith.

Dear God, I know it is easy to have faith when I have plenty. Give me faith when I have little Amen.

107. Washing the Disciples' Feet

"Then he poured water into a basin and began to wash the disciples' feet and to wipe them with the towel that was wrapped around him." - John 13:5

The Passover Festival was at hand, and it was time to celebrate the Passover meal. This is where God's people would think back to when they were in Egypt. They would remember how God passed over their children and spared their lives. They would eat a similar meal to the one God's people at those many years ago.

As the disciples sat down with Jesus to eat this meal, Jesus got up and began to wash their feet. The disciples did not know how to take this. Washing someone's feet was the lowest action you could take. That was a job for a servant, not the King. Jesus was showing them that He was a servant King. He came to serve His God and save His people.

Dear God, Teach me what it means to be a servant like Jesus. Amen.

108. Last Supper

After washing the disciples' feet, Jesus served them in another way. He served the Passover meal to them. As He did that, He explained how the Passover has always been pointing to Him. He explained that the bread that was broken and shared among them was like His body. It was going to be broken for them.

He also showed that the wine that they shared was representative of His blood. It would be spilled out, and the benefits of that would be shared among God's people. This meal is no longer called the Passover meal. It's called the Lord's Supper or Communion. It's a meal reserved for those who believe in what Jesus has done.

Dear God, The Lord's Supper is a beautiful reminder of what Jesus has done for us. I am grateful for it. Amen.

109. Judas' Betrayal

"He went away and conferred with the chief priests and officers how he might betray him to them." - Luke 22:4

In the midst of eating the Lord's Supper, Judas slipped away into the night. He had a plan in mind. He was going to betray Jesus. So, he went to the religious leaders that hated Jesus and told them that he knew where Jesus was staying tonight. He made a deal with them that if they paid him enough money, he would lead them to Jesus. They agreed and made their way to the garden where Jesus would be found.

This is a hard thing to imagine because Judas was one of Jesus' disciples. He had been following Him and helping Him for the past three years of his life. And now, he was ready to turn his back on the Savior of the world. Be warned. If such a sinful act can happen to someone so close to Jesus, it can happen in our lives too.

**Dear God, guard my heart against evil.
Give me the strength to fight the sin
and temptation in my life. Amen.**

110. Jesus prayed in the garden

"Again, for the second time, he went away and prayed, "My Father, if this cannot pass unless I drink it, your will be done." - Matthew 26:42

After finishing the Lord's Supper, they left the room they met in and walked towards the Garden of Gethsemane. They were singing as they went, worshipping God for His faithfulness in the past and now. When they arrived at the garden, Jesus told His disciples that He was going to go to a secluded place to pray. He encouraged them to do the same.

But while Jesus was praying, the disciples fell asleep three different times. Jesus continued to pray and asked God if there were any other way to save His people. The pain of the cross and the weight of the wrath of God was getting closer, and Jesus was scared. However, He didn't let that fear conquer His faith. He said, "not My will, but Yours be done."

Dear God, Jesus' example of faith in the face of fear is empowering. I pray that You would embolden my faith. Amen.

"Jesus said to him, "Friend, do what you came to do."
Then they came up and laid hands on Jesus
and seized him." - Matthew 26:50

Remember Judas, the one who was planning to betray Jesus? While the disciples were praying in the garden, he was scheming with the religious leaders. The deal was done. Judas had accepted payment and was leading them to find Jesus in the garden. He walked us to Jesus and greeted Him with a kiss. This was a sign to the soldiers of which man to arrest.

They took Him away to be put on trial. They were finally ready to accuse Him of falsely claiming to be God. They were ready to have Him killed for making those claims. The issue with their plan was that Jesus actually is God. Instead of arresting Him, they should be praising Him.

Dear God, when You sent Your Son, You knew the pain He would endure for me. Your love for me is so great. Amen.

112. Peter Denies Jesus

"Then he began to invoke a curse on himself and to swear, "I do not know the man." And immediately the rooster crowed." - Matthew 26:74

It was bad enough that Jesus had been betrayed by Judas, but a greater betrayal was coming. Peter, one of the closest friends of Jesus, denied even knowing Him shortly after His arrest. Peter was standing a good distance away from Jesus but close enough to still see Him. Three different people came up to him and said that he was one of Jesus' disciples.

Each time, Peter denied Jesus. In his last denial, he denied even knowing who Jesus was. While this hurt Jesus, this did not surprise Him. He had predicted that before the rooster crowed, Peter would deny him three times. And sure enough, the moment Peter cried out that he didn't know Jesus, the rooster crowed.

Dear God, like Peter, I have denied You and Your Son. I'm sorry for turning my back on You. Amen.

113. Jesus Crucified

"When the centurion and those who were with him, keeping watch over Jesus, saw the earthquake and what took place, they were filled with awe and said, "Truly this was the Son of God!" - Matthew 27:54

After enduring the humility of an unfair trial and the pain of beatings, Jesus carried His cross to a hill outside of the city. There He was crucified. While hanging on the cross, people continued to mock Him. There came a moment when Jesus cried out, "My God, my God, why have you forsaken me?" At that moment, Jesus gave His last breath, and everything changed.

The veil in the temple was torn in two. The earth shook. The rocks split open. The tombs were opened, and the dead were raised to life. Clearly, the death of Jesu was an earth-shattering event. One of the soldiers standing at the cross realized what he had done and confessed that Jesus actually was the Son of God.

Dear God, the death of Your Son changed everything for me. I can be saved because He took my punishment. Amen.

114. Mary Visits the Grave

"He is not here, for he has risen, as he said. Come, see the place where he lay." - Matthew 28:6

After His crucifixion, Jesus' body was taken off of the cross. A man named Joseph carried Him away and laid the body in his own grave. The grave that Jesus was laid in was not like the ones we usually see today. It wasn't a hole in the ground. It was like a little cave on the side of the hill with a large stone as a doorway.

Mary went to visit the grave and add burial spices to the body. When she arrived, she was terrified. The stone entrance to the tomb had been removed. Even more, there was an angel sitting on top of the stone. He had great news to share. He said that Jesus had been resurrected from the dead. He told Mary to run and tell His disciples.

Dear God, what an amazing ending to the story of Jesus! Death could not defeat my King! Amen.

115. Jesus is Alive

"But Peter rose and ran to the tomb; stooping and looking in, he saw the linen cloths by themselves; and he went home marveling at what had happened." - Luke 24:12

The news that Mary shared seemed too good to be true. The disciples struggled to believe it. But Peter took off running to the tomb. He had to see it for himself. Could the man that He loved and rejected really be alive again? Could Jesus have actually conquered death itself?

When he arrived, he saw the stone rolled away. He saw the empty tomb. He saw Jesus' burial cloth lay folded where the body was. It was true. Jesus died and then three days later rose again. Just as Jesus has predicted that Peter would betray Him, He predicted His own death and resurrection. And it all came true.

Dear God, I can only imagine the joy that Peter felt when he saw the empty tomb. Give me that kind of joy. Amen.

116. Jesus Meets with the Disciples

"See my hands and my feet, that it is I myself. Touch me, and see. For a spirit does not have flesh and bones as you see that I have." - Luke 24:39

Peter ran back to the disciples to tell them about the good news, and they still struggled to believe. Then something amazing happened. As the disciples were gathered in a locked room, Jesus appeared before them. Without a knock of even walking through the door, Jesus appeared in front of His disciples.

They still couldn't believe it, and so Jesus said for them to come and touch Him. He told them to come to see the nail scars in His hands and His feet and believe. Jesus really was alive again. And so, they rejoiced together with a meal. Before and after His death, Jesus shared a meal with His disciples.

Dear God, Jesus cares about His people. He cares enough to prove the truth to me. Amen.

117. Jesus Goes to Heaven

"While he blessed them, he parted from them and was carried up into heaven." - Luke 24:51

Jesus couldn't stay with His disciples forever, though. There was more work to do. Jesus stayed with His disciples for 40 days, and then He ascended into heaven. In a miraculous way that might remind you of Elijah, He was taken up into heaven. As He rose, the disciples watched until He was completely gone.

They didn't know what else to do. So, they worshipped Him. They offered up praise after praise in the temple. And then they waited. Jesus promised that He would send His Spirit to empower them one day. They didn't know how long they would have to wait, but that's exactly what they did. And then the day came. The Holy Spirit came down.

Dear God, You love me enough to never leave me alone. As Jesus went up, the Holy Spirit made His way down. Amen.

118. Pentecost

"And they were all filled with the Holy Spirit and began to speak in other tongues as the Spirit gave them utterance."
- Acts 2:4

As the disciples were waiting together for the Holy Spirit, a mighty wind came rushing through the room. As they looked around, there were tongues of fire resting on the heads of the disciples. And then, the promise was kept. The Holy Spirit filled the hearts of the disciples and gave them incredible power to share the good news.

They went out and began to tell everyone about Jesus, who was crucified, buried, and is now resurrected. While they shared this good news, the Holy Spirit gave them the ability to speak in all kinds of languages so that anyone who could listen could understand what they had to say. The gospel was beginning to spread.

Dear God, Thank You for the gift of Your Holy Spirit. I pray He will give me power today. Amen.

119. The First Church

"And they devoted themselves to the apostles' teaching and the fellowship, to the breaking of bread and the prayers." - Acts 2:42

After the Holy Spirit came down and the gospel was preached in so many languages, the greatest thing happened. People began to believe. They began to turn away from their old sinful life and follow Jesus. This group of believers was called the church. Today, we have a lot of little local churches made up of believers.

The church then and the church today are still supposed to be all about Jesus. We are supposed to be following in His baptism, eating the Lord's supper, studying His Word, and praying together in His name.

Dear God, You have given me a local church to be a part of it. Make it a church that is all about Jesus. Amen.

120. The lame man

*"[Paul] said in a loud voice, "Stand upright on your feet."
And he sprang up and began walking." - Acts 14:10*

The gospel continued to spread, and the church continued to grow. It was an incredible time for the people of God. They were teaching like Jesus, living like Jesus, and loving like Jesus. There were some who were able to do miracles like Jesus.

They were able to do miracles like healing the lame and casting out demons. These were not super-holy Christians that were granted special powers. These were Christians who God simply used to verify His message. Like when Moses was before Pharaoh and God used miracles to prove the message was true, some of the disciples were given those abilities.

Dear God, I am so encouraged to read about the rapid growth of You people. Thank You for allowing me into Your kingdom. Amen.

121. Saul to Paul

"And falling to the ground, he heard a voice saying to him, "Saul, Saul, why are you persecuting me?" - Acts 9:4

One of the incredible conversion stories that we have in the Bible is the one about Paul. Before becoming the apostle Paul, the greatest Christian missionary, he was Saul, the greatest persecution of Christians. The Bible says that Saul was still "breathing threats and murder against the disciples of the Lord" when Jesus met him face to face.

Jesus appeared in a light so bright that it temporarily blinded Saul. From that moment, Saul believed that Jesus really was the Lord. So, he took on a new name, Paul, and began to preach the gospel everywhere he went.

Dear God, if you're willing and able to use Paul, I know You can use me too. Amen.

122. Paul's Shipwreck

"But striking a reef, they ran the vessel aground. The bow stuck and remained immovable, and the stern was being broken up by the surf." - Acts 27:41

Paul's life as a missionary was not an easy one. It mirrored the life of Jesus. He continually did not have a home to sleep in, but he always had people around him. He had people like Titus and Timothy, who were his disciples. But even with good friends, Paul found himself in prison over and over again.

One of the hardest trials he faced was when he was shipwrecked on the way to another prison. A great storm came and pushed them off course. The ship hit a reef, and they were stuck. The soldiers decided they were just going to kill all of the prisoners, including Paul, and save themselves. But one soldier protected Paul.

Dear God, I cannot even imagine the struggles that Paul faced. Knowing that You protected him gives me confidence that You'll protect me too. Amen.

123. Paul's Mission

"For this reason, therefore, I have asked to see you and speak with you, since it is because of the hope of Israel that I am wearing this chain." - Acts 28:20

Paul's mission was simple. He wanted to tell God's people about their one and only hope. He wanted to tell them about Jesus. Remember all of the examples of a king, prophet, and priest from the Old Testament that fell short. Jesus is the greater and perfect version of them all.

That was what Paul tried so desperately to explain Israel. God started this whole journey towards salvation with Israel in the Old Testament, but they did not believe in Jesus. Paul pleaded with them that they would see and believe in Jesus as their only hope.

Dear God, Grow a passion in me to share about Jesus with the lost. Amen.

*"and suddenly there was a great earthquake,
so that the foundations of the prison were shaken.
And immediately all the doors were opened,
and everyone's bonds were unfastened."*
- Acts 16:26

As a final example of Paul's devotion to this mission, let me tell you a story. One time, while Paul and his friend Silas were preaching the gospel, they were arrested. They were thrown into jail like a common criminal and were left to sit there and rot. But instead of sulking and pouting, they spent the night singing praises to God.

At midnight the earth began to shake, and the doors of the prison cells flew open. Now was their chance. They could run free and continue doing the work they set out to do. But Paul wanted everyone to hear the gospel. So he waited for the jailer to find them still in the cell. He told that man about Jesus, and he believed.

Dear God, every day You provide opportunities for me to share the gospel. Help me to see them.

125. Jesus is Coming Back

"He who testifies to these things says, "Surely I am coming soon." Amen. Come, Lord Jesus!"
- Revelation 22:20

As Jesus promised His disciples before He died, He promised us again in the book of Revelation: He is coming back. He is coming back to bring full freedom and complete redemption of all things. He is coming back to judge the living and the dead. He is coming back to make all things right and all things new.

Friend, as you read this, this should be your greatest joy and surest hope. Jesus is coming back. I pray that when He does, you'll be ready to stand before Him. You won't be able to say that you've done enough good things, but you'll be able to trust that your faith in Him is good enough to save.

Dear God, I place my faith in Your Son for today and for all of eternity. Come quickly, Lord Jesus. Amen.